Still to Win

By

Sanjna S Katyal

This book is a work of non-fiction. Names and places have been changed to protect the privacy of all individuals. The events and situations are true.

ISBN: 1-4107-5937-7 (e-book)
ISBN: 1-4107-5936-9 (Paperback)

This book is printed on acid free paper.

1stBooks - rev. 05/27/03

For My Family.

"To take what there is, and use it, without waiting forever in vain for the preconceived-to dig deep into the actual and get something out of that-this doubtless is the right way to live."

Henry James

PREFACE

"STILL TO WIN" is an insight into the corporate hurricane where sometimes one experiences the spring and another times the autumn. This book is about being able to create an impact through making things happen both for oneself and for our working environment. Not giving up easily instead going that extra mile and ensuring that the sun always sets to rise again, as the night follows the day. It's about instances experienced while working with our peers or mentors or clients. Instances where we face conflict, crisis, chaos but what matters most is there is success and everyone is satisfied. There is no golden rule to making things happen but definitely there is a path to ensure that though we all make mistakes, if we can correct our doorway we might create a path for another person to walk. As also we might be able to walk together as a team one day. If we have faith, a door will always open for us, may be not the one we desired, definitely the one that will prove good for us. Sometimes we resist change but there are other times when change is for the better and it helps us to adapt a new perspective. There might not be an overnight road to success but there is a definite miracle in opportunity. As long as we can create an impact with our positive thinking and make an effort to nurture change for our working environment, we have climbed the first step to being successful as a person, as a team member and most of all as a human being. Life without taking any risk that positively impacts our social environment is like experiencing triumph without any glory. Each of us has an inherent quality that deserves to be explored, cherished and nurtured. If we experience it, happiness lies within us and it is enriched by sharing. It is the horizon of hope and our courage that strengthens us to face the unforeseen storms of time.

CONTENTS

Chapter 1

INTERVIEW NOT INTERIM VIEW

Is this not the right opportunity, the right timing for you. Yes, it is. It is an opportunity for you to explore your talent, analyze what has been your contribution to the existing and the past employers and assimilate your thought process at the right forum. This right forum is a discussion. A discussion about yourself, about the technical acumen, your personality attributes and afcourse, the organization, its business perspective, its vision and the contribution of this vision to your career.

The basic guideline to making a discussion a concrete one is to drive your interview. Be not a spectator waiting to be asked but be a captain to lead the game to victory. So the first basic thing to be a captain is to lead and know the basic rules i.e. do the home work well. Be well prepared in terms of your technical know how, your profile, and what is it you want.

Afcourse this all in one knowledge oasis comes with one word—experience. We all have experience to relate to, which means that analytical thinking helps in some way or another. It is upto you how you relate it to yourself. Strong, knowledgeable and positive self expression overpowers the entire regime of complex questions asked during a discussion. It helps to simplify the momentum of ones thought process and sharpen the broken edges of any confusion that one might have about a proven ability.

During this personal discussion it's essential to make the employer have an insight into ones accomplishments as a team player, as a leader and as a visionary. Ones technical acumen should have a sharpened edge. An ability to distinguish how different is one from the others and in what way can one contribute to the prospective organization. It is about creating an impact that lasts not for a momentary period but even when one leaves the discussion room. It is like thinking about the ghastly Ocean, the loved ones with the loss of Titanic. One need not forget the uniqueness that must highlight ones creativity and thinking.

This thought process that outlines ones contribution makes the difference. One could always narrate instances from the past where one has accomplished against tight schedules and met the client expectation. Where ones presence and the thought process have altered the sequence of events for the best. Where one is awaited to be heard cautiously by everyone in the team.

Do let the prospective employer know what your areas of improvement are. It is always better to put the cards on the table and then talk. Your areas to improve should be in the light of your eagerness to change, which actually highlights your flexibility as a person. Mention about your personality attributes that have helped you towards this road to knowledge. Where you have taken the initiative to bring change in yourself. Instances where you can actually set example for the other person to think, to learn and may be to adapt your learning methodology.

As easy it is to highlight the personality strength, much complex it is to highlight ones not so strong personality attributes. It takes courage to accept ones shortcomings with a smile. Accepting with confidence that one can overcome these, on the ground where final job decisions have to be made is an uphill task. To convince oneself that we all have our shortcomings and homosapiens is not meant to be a perfect species is challenging. It's essential to know about oneself, an insight that helps us appreciate ones own ability which makes us frown at times.

Never hesitate to say "no." No does not signify disqualification but your acceptance of facts about which you need to improve upon. It's unrealistic to be the "know-all" in every discipline. Admitting that one is widely aware about every blossom blooming during the spring, puts anyone in doubt. Knowledge is all about improving and learning. That's how one grows on a learning curve. Knowledge is best learnt with mutual sharing and not keeping it boxed. One is not expected to know everything also, else there would be only teachers and no student left to learn.

Be presentable. Remember you are here to create an impact. An impact about yourself and there is just one single product you are marketing - yourself. It's about packaging yourself with colorful streamers and candles that brightens a darkened room when lit. It's about being oneself, about whom you know almost everything and there are no surprises to follow. A complementary feature is being energetic and responsive in thinking. It's about selling an idea, a product of intellect and humor that can sharpen the existing system in an organization.

Be confident when you meet with people, an eye contact is necessary because in a face-to face communication, eye contact plays an important role. It signifies confidence. You might not realize it, but your body language is being closely monitored as a barometer would monitor the weather! Remember it's all happening at the same time so you need to be careful in expressing yourself. The entire mechanism of self expression is being examined through an eagle's eye view, which you might not realize immediately.

Ask focused questions, about the organization, the work, the job responsibilities, the career growth opportunities etc. Remember time is money and both the employer and your self are investing time on each other. So make the most of this opportunity, opportunity for you to talk about yourself. Is that not fun?

Speak always but at the right forum. Never undermine yourself or be aggressively competitive. This in context to compensation. It is always better to know the way the market is moving and mention your expectation at the same time. After all you are here to seek a better career and have monetary gains with benefits. So it is essential to know the market trends at your level.

Be careful when you are giving the reference. You must be sure that the reference is people with whom you have proved yourself and have the confidence in you. Although this might be the last stage of the selection process but can always be a decisive one. It can turn the tables in decision making if one is not cautious.

Selecting the job is a complete package of work environment, job responsibilities, compensation and benefits, career growth. No one factor would determine the job selection. Be shrewd in thinking about everything before you make a change. Only one factor inducing you to change might be a hygiene factor for a shorter duration. Infact explore about the new company. Do make an in-depth study on the role being assigned, the opportunity available, how the market is reacting to the organization, is there any stability or are you simply taking a risk. If you are taking a risk is it worth the effort. After all it's about your career and you have the right to know.

You might experience a sense of uneasiness if you are unable to respond to all the questions asked. Let us not forget the basic guideline that is, the fruits of knowledge are best learnt when shared. One cannot be expected to know everything all the time. However what ever one knows should be assimilated and expressed with clarity, brevity and precision. One might experience a different perspective shared with the interviewer over a variety of questions asked. Let's not forget, if everyone thought alike there would be monotony in learning. It is essential to have ones own opinion but with a little flexibility of acceptance to listen to another persons view point. Being like the arrow that knows where to target the object helps to maintain the right focus.

Ample times one wonders about the final outcome which might be communicated at a latter stage. However the consequences of the effort should not be disheartening because one can never do beyond ones best. Surely it is essential and satisfying to get a favorable response to ones effort but its equally essential to appreciate that missing one opportunity should not crumble ones ambition. Instead it should be a stepping stone to challenge ones own potential, to ensure the next time the response is positive and welcoming.

Always remember in a personal discussion the word "failure" does not exist. It's the difference of perception that drives a decision favorably or unfavorably. It is critical but not the be all or the end all nor is it an end in itself. We all know that no two people can always think alike on every matter. They should not else every problem would have a similar solution and there would be no variation in thinking. Everything would be in black or white don't we need colors to spice our life?

So here you are to champion your thought process, to deliver your talent, to market your skills, to design a career path for yourself. Here you are moulding things keeping your interest and the business perspective in mind. The best part is-its all about you. So blow your trumpet. Does it not feel good to know that here are people eager to know about you! Does it not feel special that you get an opportunity to assimilate your knowledge into a nest of spontaneity and confidence? It is all about your own aspiration and most of all it is about yourself. So paint the canvas as colorful as you desire but do not forget to give it the final touches of intellect, humor and reason.

Chapter 2

MEETING THE NUMBER GAME

Hiring quality people with the best academic record and suitable skills has always been an uphill task. It imbibes challenge and at times frustration. Manpower planning is not an easy task with the best candidates knowing they "can make it happen by choice." It is not about anyone getting a job anywhere, it's about the best getting the job at the best companies. Now what "the best" is becomes hard to define.

Is it all about money, attitude, environment, planning a career, international exposure, challenge, benefits or is it that strong pillar that compiles it all and is called "PIECAMB." No one factor could attract the right person for the right job be it money or environment and least of all merely benefits.

In such a competitive market what does Ishan, the Human Resources Manager at Force Link do. The past hiring strategies have not attracted the best, definitely the hiring numbers have been met, but this does not deter the technical manager to complain all the time, everytime. He needs the opportunity to begin and he goes endlessly complaining about what the "human resources should" and what the "human resources should not." So Ishan definitely has a problem to solve that needs time, patience and most of all the goodwill of the policy believers.

The traditional media strategy was a fiasco, so was the web advertising or job fair. The internal referral program was inspiring but could not make its mark as expected. Though the reference fee was lavish but did not enable him to reach the target as desired. The rolling ball of problem was getting the quality people. For months the organization was feeding its belly with good technical professionals from good institutes but not the best from the best institutes.

Having tried each strategy, Ishan wondered what to do? Nothing seemed to practically work and the pressure from the technical managers could burst as a balloon anytime; making an unnecessary chaos and creating panic in the organization. There was work but not the best people to perform and deliver; there was a target but not enterprising people with initiative.

Tired with the daily chaotic monotony at work with number game, one weekend, he decided to visit the Plymouth Cultural festival. This festival was known for the diversity of cultures it attracts and offered an immense variety especially theatre. As also Force Link was sponsoring the entire theatre show. This was a last minute decision and everyone in the organization was convinced that it was a sheer waste of time. "The technical gurus have nothing to do with theatre and entertainment, they can't see beyond coding and a computer screen," screamed his manager. Ishan faced an opposition from everywhere in the organization. His idea surprised the technical managers and they wondered if the organization required another human resources manager.

After a long battle Ishan was able to convince his manager that hiring is creativity and its success depends on exploring and not in traditional methods. It was never easy for Ishan to get the Human resources budget approved on activities which involved a different methodology and creativity that spelled a different language. But Ishan made it happen for once. He knew he had taken a risk, he knew he had to justify his stand and most of all he fully understood that failure was not an option.

So Ishan headed towards the Plymouth cultural festival. He collected the entire stock of visiting cards and drove 80 miles away. His CRV had a big banner on it "Force link is hiring -call 697-654-1651 or email ishan@forcelink.com." Though his van gave a comic resemblance but it was meant to create the impact, to be different, to bring a change.

Would it ever bring a change, he was doubtful because this act was being slightly wild. However he knew he had to ensure he is successful else his job would be at stake. As it is, meeting the hiring numbers was becoming a key concern in his appraisal. So it was a "make or break" situation for him.

It was the first time he was going to the Plymouth festival. The idea was to be creative and to enjoy. However at the back of his mind he knew, if this exercise was a fiasco, his manager would ruin his happiness. The technical managers would make him miserable also. More so the next day of the festival was the management meeting where Ishan had to share his experience and show results. He had no choice but to deliver successfully.

While he stepped into the festival he dint know where to start from. The décor was exciting and young. Would he ever meet a single technical person in such a festival was doubtful. For a moment he thought he made a mistake by coming to the festival. He should have probably advertised for the positions as done in the past. Somehow he could not convince himself to believe that he could be successful.

After few hours being his natural self, he decided to enjoy and participate in almost every event. For a moment he did not want to think about the number game. He wanted to explore and understand the place, the people and the surroundings.

To his surprise, while at the festival he interacted with a number of technical savvy gurus. The festival offered this opportunity by means of games, water sports, dining and drinking. He participated rather aggressively in each of them. Exchanging the visiting cards was merely an introductory mode of starting a conversation. The initial idea was just to know each other. For sometime he had forgotten about hiring, about the office chaos, the hiring panic, the number game. He mingled, enjoyed, had fun, made friends, learnt about different cultures and decided to move on. After an eventful day he headed back simply with good memories. He enjoyed himself to the fullest.

On his way back home, the hiring trauma haunted him. He knew he was answerable to his management team. He also knew that he had to be result oriented to justify his visit to the festival. He was unsure if the fruit would ripe within a day. How come he had completely forgotten about the number game. It dint strike him even for a minute, as he was fully engrossed with people around him.

However he was sure that with people he met he had created an impact. He was able to express himself well, though he never mentioned about hiring spree to most of them. He never mentioned to them that he could help them seek a job opportunity in Force Link. He was too focused on understanding their interests and exploring their talent. He did not implore about their academic records or their technical or functional skills. Ishan was convinced that he was about to face a disaster the next day. Should he take leave and stay away, he wondered. How would he confront his technical managers and most of his mentor?

Little did Ishan realize the next day his inbox was overflowing with mails? He was sure that these mails were from his technical managers or his mentor who was waiting for Ishan to respond about his visit to Plymouth and the disaster it had caused. He was sure that these were mails he dint want to read. He wished that the server had crashed or these mails could be automatically deleted before even being read.

To his sheer surprise these were from the Plymouth event. Few were friends but the majorities were job seekers. Each of them appreciated his focus on their creative thinking. It made them feel he was unique and attempted to understand a person in totality. Someone who would not segment himself into the percentile knowledge. Who could see beyond an algorithm or a technical code.

He was relieved and knew how to handle things now. He would have his way to ensure he is successful the way he wants and how he wants. Enough of dictations from the technical managers or his own mentor. Ishan took the lead. The response surprised the managers at the meeting, none expected. Everyone wondered how did this happen. The strategy was simple and the results encouraging. So were the earlier methods of hiring not suitable to the current times or the strategy adopted by Ishan was most fruitful. He did not create a miracle in his strategy. Instead he tried to follow a methodology in a unique manner where work was fun, where there was a wholesome ingredient of joy and a feeling of completion. Where there was passion and challenge, risk and uncertainty.

Ishan explained his managers how critical creativity and creating impact helped. Hiring is not jut a number game to meet the project deadlines but it's a creative mode of exploring talent in a different scenario. Knowing people in their "less formal self" was much more interesting and challenging. It enabled him understand people, their interests, their aspirations and most of all a wholesome entity who was thriving to achieve a dream.

Interacting with people just as they are, evolved a chemistry of knowledge that was worth sharing, appreciative and admirable. It might be a coincidence that he was successful but it was not a coincidence that 'he made things happen." He ensured to bring a new perspective to "meeting the number game" not just for this day but for times to come. Simply because being creative helps.

At times one has to see beyond the boxed processes and procedures that entangle our freedom of thought. He might not have adopted the best strategy possible but he definitely took the initiative to focus with ample believe in himself.

Chapter 3

BEING POSITIVE NOW AND ALWAYS

The reason most people never reach their goals is that they don't define them, or ever seriously consider them as believable or achievable. "Winners can tell you where they are going, what they plan to do along the way, and who will be sharing the adventure with them", Denis Watley.

It's never late to arise and rethink on your plans. We all come across varied degrees of problems each hour of each day, but the beauty lies in, not the escape mechanism, but facing them with a positive perspective. It is so easy to talk about 'being positive' midst a problem at office or at home. Do problems not first create chaos in mind, uneasiness, the why you and not anyone else syndrome? Let's not forget we are here in this world to share the load of Success and failure, not Success alone and mind you, neither failure alone.

It is a mix of both. A taste of sugar with a pinch of salt. However, how does one stay positive about oneself and about others? With the everyday growing politics at work, with colleagues trying to walk away with credit that hurts, with a boss who is intentionally ignorant about your Expertise, gathers your ideas and claims as his? It might not happen always but it definitely happens sometimes.

Yes, it is possible. It is possible to be positive midst all this chaos and it is "you" who has to make it happen. Noone else but you. You have to arise above the rest to help yourself. Remember no one will help; everyone out there is a great advisor because advising is the easiest. It is just a game of words people play. You have to fight your own battle and win for yourself. Do not wait.

For lady luck to smile at ease, it might not happen for months together.

Here is the rule game that you might want to follow at work. You could always differ on this but these are few decisive moments.

The most essential thing is being honest to yourself and being convinced you gave the best. However you promise yourself that incase of any correction, you would acknowledge it and improve. Incase you need to defend yourself, you must. Never let the world take you for a ride. It all begins with you and ends with us. It is not always about "me" and "mine" instead it is about "we" and "us."

Expose your talent, when you must and at the right time, with the right forum and the right place. Let people out there know you exist. Let your knowledge speak for you. It is equally important to expose this knowledge to the outer world-at office, during presentations, during meetings, during one-to-one meetings with the mentor. Just remember unless you have spoken you stand unheard since you have not expressed it. One doesn't mean to go into the battlefield armed with weapons, all ready to shoot. You are not being asked to bomb the field instead be always ready to conquer.

Be spontaneous. Yes, it is an art. It does not come as easily like a complementary gift at the Christmas sale. However, you need to become the Santa Claus sometimes. With the onset of Christmas, you know the children expect out of you. Similarly try developing a habit of being alert while things are happening. Once you are spontaneous, you get an edge over others in self-expression. Do you know what else you achieve? You achieve recognition and fast recognition. So much so, that during a meeting, all eyes would be facing you for a constructive suggestion. It is all because you are a rolling mill of ideas. Ideas come best when you talk a lot to people, when you share experiences, when you are well read, when you know the latest, when you can feel the heat of the moment-that is how ideas come. You actually have to make a deliberate effort.

Be confident and do not let anything disturb your confidence. Confidence is most important. Never let your morale down or get discouraged. Project deadlines, client dissatisfaction, lack of skills to deliver are positively concern areas. These are challenges you need to face. Instead not bring you uncalled stress that is what Lack of confidence is all about. Look at the past and tell yourself the success stories related to your career and help yourself to build a rising spirit of confidence.

Learn to mind your own business. Remember we all are in the corporate world to compete, to prove against each other who are the best? At the same time we have principles of team work, co-operation, and mutual give and take to follow. We all are smart people with respect to our abilities. Over years, we have learnt the good and the bad of the corporate world. As a good co-worker, a mentor or a subordinate take the initiative to value add. Once again at the right forum and with the right people.

Do not get yourself frustrated fast, learn to be patient. You might be a doer in one project doing a hard-core operational activity you hate to perform; you might also be a manager in the next project leading the project. Give yourself and the organization the time to think for each other. The worst that frustration can do is it compels you to "give up" and bring toll of stress with the worst in you. It is not worth the exercise. Instead of packing your bags, cool down. You deserve much more than all this stress. Why be impatient. After all you have a proven record of success. Remember smart work and hard work always pays. Nothing goes waste; it is a matter of time.

Meditation helps. It helps your mind and body to relax and think in peace. It helps you to be at peace with yourself, with the matter around you. It helps you to collate your experiences and act positively. It will help your internal system to rest. This is important. You might feel it is a waste of time but its not. It is all the more important as it is about you.

Create an Impact. Yes, this comes with experience but it is the key to meet success with your thoughtful thinking. Let people know that you are a person with a lot of difference you create and make the difference with your knowledge and initiative.

Talk to your mentor when you get the opportunity. Share with him your success and your ideas, your thought process, but never your shortcomings. It's human to grasp the weakness of a personality easier than learn to appreciate. Appreciation comes with lots of effort. Let your mentors know what you are doing; don't wait for him to ask you.

Stop Cribbing and start thinking. Thinking on a positive note midst the worst possible situation can alone offer solutions. Thinking on a cribbing note midst the worst possible situation will churn out the worst possible solution also. Cribbing is self-pity. One reason why you offer yourself self-pity? What should have happened cannot be erased because it is imploring past, what could happen, is future unseen. What can happen is your control point. So, concentrate on that. Cribbing is escape mechanism it helps you to visualize events the way you perceive and that you are right in your perception.

So why not be positive. Act positive and think positive. Why let negative forces disturb your work and mind, without reasons. Problems will come, but you are smart, intelligent, competent and ambitious-you ought to have a complete formula towards a solution. In the war of ideas, you are the Parent, Adult, and the Child **in** the same situation. Cool down, relax, and give yourself a breathing point. You are also the fighter, the creator, and the master of yourself.

With such supreme qualities **in** your personality; how can anything as little as any problems disturb you? Sure, midst stress it is hard to find a ventilation of joy, midst lack of role clarity at job its hard to appreciate job enrichment and job satisfaction, with being left behind, when you shouldn't have been, is upsetting. Still worst is no one ready to appreciate your viewpoint.

Do not forget the most important person is "you." It begins and ends with you.

You can create the impact, the difference, the change; you can above all make things happen because you believe in taking the challenge. It is because you live, you breathe, you execute, you believe by positive thinking.

"Most people ask for happiness on condition. Happiness can only be felt if you don't set any condition." Arthur Rubinstein

Chapter 4

THE GRILLING CHICKEN

What do you remember the best from your personal discussion with the prospective employer? Did it bring an insight into your thought process, did it evolve an unsaid mechanism of enthusiasm in you, or did you feel a waste of time! For a moment did you feel you were being grilled in the heat of thoughts?

You made a mistake visiting the company and you would avoid doing so for times to come. But what exactly happened -was it favorable or unfavorable or you don't care as you are exhausted by the process itself? It is grilling but that is what it was meant to be. You are the subset to the set called organization and you together have to complement each other. It's like the two pillars of "knowledge in action" supporting each other.

A discussion is the forum for your opinion and your judgment about opportunity you tried. It is also a mechanism to gauge the market trends. It is also an insight into oneself. What does one do, once you are back from such a grilling selection process? Should such a war of ideas create an impact?

To start with simply relax. Give yourself the opportunity to be in solace before you compel yourself to explode into an unforgiving frustration. It's easy to relish the fruit of success and not easy to taste the bitter wrath of failure sometimes. It's worst if one is left unattended by both success and failure, and is left to wonder will anything materialize at all. That is sometimes the claws of uncertainty can cause uneasiness.

Let your system naturally assimilate the mode of events. To leave things open ended. After all nothing is an end in itself, it is only a means to an end. Events enable us think, sometimes the range of ideas is shallow another times as deep as the sea. There might be no striking resemblance between the deep sea and the shallow water except both follow a consistent momentum with the rising tide. Both lighten with the horizon and are silent during the night.

So how does one define what is critical? Does one not care about the opportunity lost? Alternatively, to keep imploring about it will neither help because you are not the decision-maker. You are on the "other side of the table." Aren't you? So what do you do? Here you are wondering, will you be selected or not. Sometimes trying to put it at the back of your mind and trying to forget about it. Leaving things as they are let these take the natural course. Or you don't care because there are enough opportunities in the market which might be false perception for oneself until one explores.

We all sense a comfort level in our cushioned thoughts until we challenge them, unless there is a driving conflict that inspires us to rethink. As long as the pathway is clear our spinning confidence moves ahead without a hault. But what does one do when the path is unclear and doubtful. Do we hault never to proceed further or do we carve a way that enables us to steer forward?

Stop worrying and start thinking. If you said it to yourself, you gave the best, it summarizes everything. Become pragmatic about events, an opportunity gained is as much a gamble as an opportunity lost.

Remember success is 50% perspiration, 30% inspiration and 20% Luck. You can always add or subtract the variables according to your conviction. Give yourself another opportunity to explore your talent.

Never let your morale down and anything discourage you. Just because events did not click favorably does not imply one has lost. Never ever forget for a moment, you are the best. You are talented, creative, intelligent and smart. Each of us have a creative ability to perform; each of us has a distinguished thought process to achieve the best. As long as we are making a focused effort to achieve our objectives, we will succeed. Concrete focus and sincere effort are inherent seeds to nurture the fruits of success. It might not happen this moment or even a week from now, but definitely there will be success in future.

The most important of all is learning. Learn from your experience. Nothing teaches you better than life will. Most of all you invested time to understand the organization the organization took time to understand you. Therefore, what would create a win - win situation? Once a while through such events analyzing oneself is an interesting activity. Measuring the ocean of strength against the rising tide of weaknesses can be a thrilling insight into oneself. These are instances that give us a phenomenal opportunity to bring a change for the better. Surely change is not easy and it nurtures resistance at times. However it enables us to improve for the best sometimes. It might not bless us with immediate success but it definitely will help us understand ourselves.

Rising above the swamp of confusion into the mirage of reality can help us surmount our own doubts.

Post discussions after an interview I feel is an excellent opportunity for you to analyze yourself and work towards a change for the better if taken supporting. No matter what your experience is, improving oneself for the better is an ongoing learning. The best part is you do a value addition to yourself. You are helping yourself to become the best; you are giving yourself the opportunity not once but several times. Whether you are selected or not is immaterial to the extend of making a sincere attempt to achieve. Knowledge is about constant learning, one cannot be expected to be a champion in every field.

But one is expected to be a champion in some of the fields. The question is not about who is right and what is wrong i.e. you correctly answered but the organization lacked the maturity to understand your perception. It is about change, about learning, about improving oneself, it is not simple words, it is action.

It is challenging because it's a deep rooted insight into oneself. It can be overwhelming because our expertise is being questioned, analysed and examined within the boundaries of our own intellect. However self—analysis should be a supportive and not a disturbing process.

Self Analysis is an opportunity to learn and understand where we need to improve. It is not an attempt to disown those unpleasant habits which are hindering our way to do well in life. Neither is it an opportunity to cover up for our own short comings. One can stand midst the array of excuses and constantly justify oneself for every event that goes wrong. Alternatively one can pierce through the narrow edges of conflict and contemplate how to improve. How to make things happen for oneself not for today but for each upcoming moment. Who does not want to be a winner?

What's important is you made an attempt, a sincere attempt and you succeeded because success is not always about winning, success is about winning and learning while losing. It is about change that glitters your thought process and compels you to improve. So much so that you assure yourself never to repeat the unwanted. It is about the confidence you instill in yourself. What a contribution you have made to yourself, is it not amazing. You learnt while you tried. You tried while you were sure. You were sure because you were clear. You were clear because you were confident. You are confident because you believe in yourself. You are a real winner, aren't you? "Be not angry that you cannot make others as you wish them to be, since you cannot make yourself as you wish to be." Thomas a Kempis

Chapter 5

DOING WELL BUT DIFFERENTLY

Loaded in this heap of files, with series of meeting on her planner and clients to visit, sometimes she wonders -why twenty four hours make the day -so short lived. In the professional career she has left no stone unturned to make things happen for both -the organization and her professional well being. It's partially satisfying, this entire gamut of smart working with a "do what it takes attitude." It's stimulating, encouraging and fulfilling. She aspires to reach the paradise of perfection one day, to experience the wholesome nectar of success.

Life looks incomplete until she visits the office, has done some fire fighting on project management, pierced through few rough days; that's what keeps her alive. It's all in her flesh and blood-meeting with client satisfaction. Marketing new ideas, basically being the best -as she believes - either you are ahead of the game or you are out of it.

She cannot allow any one to overstep her ideas. She has been fortunate never to sense the wrath of failure. Her confidence inspires her to spearhead the rest. She has learnt to lead without thinking twice about the consequences. Surely she is in a hurry. She is entangled in a web where it's not easy for her to pause and relax. She does not have the time to rethink because she likes to overpower.

She has implemented the best projects so far, no one can beat her ranking in customer satisfaction. She has brought the best possible business for the organization and knows how to delegate responsibility. She is considered excellent in people, project and client management. Her art of working is unique; her style to deliver distinguishes her from the gurus in her field. She is young but has seniors reporting to her on the project. She is envied and loved.

If she looks back -this is what she is all about -with fifteen hours of work each day, she wakes up again to catch with everything but herself. She has traveled intensely. She has met the leaders in the industry. She knows how to sieve the better from the best. She knows it all but about her inner self.

Here is Radha, wanting to make things happen in life and expecting the best out of life. Yes she is the beauty and the brain but who is Radha -no one knows. Her boss knows she is a staunch professional, her colleagues understand her as a technical savvy person, and her clients rate her best. She is different. She is akin to the blossom in the spring one would yearn to grow in the courtyard.

However despite this success, Radha senses an incompletion in her personality today. Something she can share with nobody. Since long she is finding herself lost somewhere. There are no answers but only questions.

She seems to be drowning in this ocean of chaos where sailing is difficult. She is unable to confront for once, these rising tides compelling her to explore about herself. However she lacks a sense of satisfaction that completes a person. She is unable to experience an eternal sense of happiness despite incessant success at work. Surely there is a driving focus to work and to achieve but there is a cloud of queries surmounting her. She has begun to frown today. She is in a state of mind where she is caught between the storms that is severe and compelling. Should she take a break from work, she doesn't know. Should she lessen the pace of work, she wonders. Should she stop traveling -she is confused! Is she trying to climb the pinnacle of her ambition in too little time? Why is she in such a hurry she cannot comprehend?

She is cheerful and fun loving -she is everything but herself today.

She is on a pathway where she cannot return to restart. She fully understands that she is heading towards a destination that bestows her success. However there is an inbuilt urge to seek internal happiness. Her thoughts are well carved with intellect and humor but she is unable to compile them in totality. She seemed to be well conquered by this internal conflict. Neither can she escape nor can she detach herself from these thoughts. She cannot isolate herself from this internal strife that echoes each moment in her today. The more she ploughs, the more she is perplexed.

She is craving for a solution that is well knitted in reason and facts. With this ongoing outburst she has begun to become restless and thoughtful. In this struggle for self identify, she has left an important part of herself behind. Little does she realize that it has been ages since she painted the canvas with her thoughtful colors?

The colors have soiled, the canvas is nowhere closer to her imagination any more and the brushes have long broken. But this is what she started with -her creative self. Where has it all gone? It's unseen beneath the dusty heap of schedules, meetings and fire fighting. There is no time for her to bind herself together with her creative self. But that's an integral part of her personality which she cannot afford to alienate.

However in this everyday struggle which she enjoys there is ample stress. Stress that's eating up her system, not letting her be -what she wants to and how she wants to. These are the gimmicks of the corporate world, may be. She shares but with herself how tired she is with these long travels. Airport looks as the second home now. She might be fed up of this routine but has little options before herself. What must she do to keep herself alive?

No sooner she realized one day, she needs to prioritize her time. She ought to devote time to herself and think beyond project schedule and customer. She has risen and will rise -considering she is talented and intelligent. But she was imploring about the missing link with herself. The bond that completes her in totality and nourishes her intellect with happiness. Where there is no stress or despair and only satisfaction. Where she is able to complete herself as a person. Where ambition is well measured with satisfaction and happiness and not success alone.

That evening while back from work, Radha brought the broken brushes together, she cleared the dusty canvas and started to color. At the first place, she drew about those instances in office that were disturbing her all the time. However she was not satisfied with her work. So she started again to paint. On a fresh canvas she began to paint without thinking about work, the daily chaos, and the worrying incidents. She began to mix such beautiful colors together and she started to create something of her own.

Something which she was not experiencing everyday and it was completely original. Slowly as time passed Radha started to play with these colours, she began to sense a deep feeling of happiness after ages. She began to realize in a very short time that these colors made her feel overjoyed.

Slowly she began to realize that the *"missing link"* in her life was her creative self. Which she was forgetting about. Where she needs to pay attention as well. Which is an integral part of her life -it's on the canvass where she expresses herself the best. The board meetings are business driven, the project deadlines are customer driver -but these colors, the expressions, this happiness she gathers, the solace she gets -is totally self-driven.

What she learnt that evening was -her creativity is an important part to her personality, where she needs to give time. No matter how busy the schedules are, she cannot afford to lose herself -in that endless traveling. She cannot forget about herself in the process of self-grooming. Thereafter she promised herself never to forget these colors she cherishes. Therefore, she started to sketch landscape while on plane, so she started to paint the sunset with the fall colors. She began to once again live life her way!! Doing well but this time doing it differently.

Chapter 6

TWO STEPS BEHIND

Today the Business Survey held yearly by the organization, awards her for the excellence in people management. A piece of success that anyone in hierarchy would like to grab and own it.

Her dynamism and intellect surprises her superiors, her peers smile with envy. How can anyone learn from someone so young and rule out the "grey hair advice one wonders."

The reality seemed hard to reconcile with but facts speak for themselves. The best in the field in the organization wondered but were convinced about her abilities, her technical acumen, her result driven temperament and above all the personal touch she brings. Her critiques are convinced she deserves this success.

Vaidhi is simple and soft, smart working and sharp. She is cautious, knows what she is doing and what she wants. She is practicing what some of us talk about and advise others to execute.

She ensured she attends every training program organized in soft skills but those are theoretical jargons. Basic concepts we all have heard about not once but these keep drumming into our ears. That is just an awareness-building program -so why would consultants want to work with her? Why would she be rated the best? How has she endured and survived. Her critiques ensured her projects don't go live but they do against all odds right on time, the customer believes by her always.

Vaidhi has her reasons to be successful. Success has been a slippery mountain to climb where she has fallen ample times. But she knows that you climb a mountain one step at a time. She admits today that nothing happens overnight; one has to work towards being patiently successful. It was "people" who were hard to handle, she knew it was a challenge, sometimes a frustrating one.

She was given a project in troubled waters and a team that was above average and not from the best technology schools. Did it mean a lot of handholding, patience, conviction that one can deliver and above all, building from the scratch? That was not true. The team though above average comprised smart and sharp thought process with a willingness to learn. The task before her was to ensure they are completely result driven.

One thing she ensured all this while was—her team should not lose its focus. It was clear and every member knew what they were doing. She developed in them the confidence that was acquired over a period of time.

She gave her team the space to grow, to decide for themselves. This decentralization helped each member to develop a sense of ownership. Along with ownership, she gave them the authority within their periphery.

There were times when important presentations to the customer were handled by the team members and not her. That is because she wanted to give them visibility. She wanted to position them rightly, so that the customer identifies the right resources for the right task.

It started with the initial chaos but ended fruitfully. The customer knew whom to ask-what, when, where and how. She knew as long as this was taken care, they would deliver.

She wanted each member to participate in important decision-making exercises for the project. This helped them to "think aloud" She experience excellent inputs from the teammates and this helped in the overall progress of each module implementation.

Yes, she was able to keep her team intact not only at work but outside. Team get togethers became a common feature in the group. The group enjoyed being with each other and welcoming folks from other projects as well. The right occasions were celebrated at the right time and she joined hands with each member when she experienced problems being faced.

She ensured none in the team feels isolated. No two members are alike but each is competent and a "go - getter" They have to be groomed accordingly. The academic grooming has taken care of their conceptual being; all they needed was the practical side to this knowledge.

She encouraged her team members to "speak-up." This did not mean complaining or grumbling; instead it meant to lessen ones load of thoughts. It meant to correct a thought process bringing discomfort. It meant to lighten the load of anxiety.

Above all, she had faith in her people. She knew they could make it happen. She instilled in them the confidence to make it happen. Some how the project in trouble waters was becoming a challenge everyday; to prove to oneself that success was becoming important each day. Things started changing. The project was going on time and the team was fully sure to go live at the set date. There was no scope for any delay, and above all the customer was becoming positive.

Eventually she was the most talked about person by the employees. None frowned at her team anymore. What she was practicing was basic working style with a difference. What was bringing the difference was her personality. Her temperament that her success lies in the success of her people. In such a self - focused environment at the corporate level, she was here to create an impact-a positive impact that balances people and business together. No one can be viewed in isolation.

She knows there was enough grape vine in the organization opposing her openness at work. Her young dynamism brought discomfort to her superiors. Did her aggressive global traveling brought forth these basic ideas at work, or was it her ability to adapt and change that made the difference. Was it her caring temperament or her ability to consciously improve herself -they would wonder! The fact that she delivered at the right time silenced all doubts. The customer feedback was enough to justify the effort and teamwork.

Vaidhi is here to prove that -no mater what, no matter why, no matter how-success shared is success enjoyed and positivism reinforces the belief in oneself. Its none but oneself, one needs to convince to makes things happen, the rest falls in place not automatically but with persistent effort. "All things are possible until they are proved impossible-and even the impossible may only be so, as of now." Pearl S Buck.

Chapter 7

THE BEARING POINT

Well what is the problem here -does the mentor not understand Vishi or is Vishi too smart and intelligent for him. With a bad economy, no growth prospects in the organization, not a very lucrative salary-where does Vishi go. Does she quit or does she lock herself in this overall stressful environment. Stress not due to deadlines but stress due to lack of opportunity. To add to the hurricane, Vishi has been pointed out on her 'communication skills." A rough weather with mentor and here is Vishi being nominated for the "communication skills program."

Vishi brings to table sixteen years of experience; she has been a sales guru back in her country. In the past, her clients praised her for her talent, her creativity and most of all her ability to market the product. So what went wrong in this damn place - Canada? It's totally driven her nuts.

Well taking her mentors feedback supportingly, she attended the training program. She clearly pointed to the training faculty the issue was not "communication" well it was "cultural diversity." The diversity was the focus of attention and that's essential to her. Though the training finished but Vishi knew at the back of her mind-she would surely not be a front runner in the sales team as long as she stays in Canada or atleast as she is working with "The stratums." Would she be able to overcome this labeled barrier of communication? She knew changing her mentor's perception would be a challenge for her, which might lead to a stunted growth for her also.

She was doing the level two activities since the day she joined "The Stratums." She called them "level two activities" because she was asked to get involved in assignments which she performed ages back in her career. Was joining this organization a mistake, was she foolish enough not to appreciate that "cultural diversity" could play havoc with her career. What went wrong that such a successful person saw a downward curve in career growth?

The job role discussed with her at the time of selection was surely about being on the forefront of the sales team. So how come, everything drowned into the slump so quickly. Sales was her first love, she enjoys it and she just can't sit preparing presentations for her mentor all the time. It's pathetic and disgusting, she felt to herself.

Vishi spend ample time imploring her career growth. Nothing seemed to materialize and the option to quit without a good opportunity at hand was not wisdom. Leaving Canada for another country without an opportunity was equally crazy. So what does she do?

Vishi patiently continued with her everyday job. At the same time in the evenings she used to dig out her sales contacts or make cold calls. She began to meet with her old clients and explained them the nature of the business, the value addition this product could make to their organization. In the beginning her plan was a real fiasco. Things didn't seem that bright as one would imagine. Well all doesn't happen the way one wants!

To some extend, things were becoming frustrating for Vishi.

She was losing control over things, her patience with constant failure was declining, she was getting tired of being the "second level clout" in the organization-this is not what she deserved. Or would it continue as this from now on.

Knowing Vishi, she is not here to accept hail storm all the time, the sun has to shine over her roof. She continued to contact her previous clients and make cold calls.

One fine evening she met her prospective client and had a discussion about the products sold by "The Stratums." Yes she was able to position the brand and that was a feather in her cap. Next morning, Steve her prospective client called and decided to go ahead with the detailed presentation to the management team by Vishi.

Vishi discussed about this meeting with her mentor. It surprised him totally. At the back of his mind, he was sure that this deal would not work out. He was confident that Vishi was no good a presenter. She would not make it at all. However he asked her to proceed with her plan. There is always a "may be" in the sales game plan; there is always a twist to the number game. However he made it a point attending this presentation.

So January 20th, was a critical day for Vishi. Steve was confident she would be able to sell the deal, as against the thoughts of her mentor. Steve knew, Vishi has a talent to sell, to make the difference, she was no ordinary person, and she was there to make her mark. She always was in his words the "sales guru." However his management had to take a call and not him.

All this while, her mentor wondered why he let Vishi go ahead with this meeting.

It could be a real disaster, he was sure to walk out of the room uncertain, confused and in sheer failure. But he had no choice as Vishi insisted and disagreed with him on all his points that dissuaded her to present. It surprised him because that was unlike her. More so it was her initiative. And suppose the deal was successful, "The Just In Time" would be a cash cow client for his organization.

So started Vishi's presentation. Her statistics, the tone of her style, the in-depth knowledge, the ability to put her point, surprised the management team at "The Just In Time." They were not only convinced by her viewpoint but also congratulated her for making an excellent value addition. Yes they were convinced about the one million dollar deal. They realized the product would benefit the entire organization and the way Vishi put it, anyone would be convinced. The deal was signed.

So here was Vishi bringing success to table and reviving the lost game. She created a deep impact on everyone. She made the difference, no doubt. She made it happen, for the first time before a mentor who lacked the ability to acknowledge her expertise.

Vishi was congratulated by her mentor for the success. He was appreciative of her abilities. Her success surprised him; her talent left a deep impact on him. However Vishi could feel a sense of guilt in him. She dint speak much, her success was learnt by everyone in the organization. She was the most talked about person in the organization; she was there to set an example to the organization.

So what was the problem implored her mentor, was it "communication" or was it his lack of ability to appreciate a diversified working environment which he himself had never either experienced or appreciated.

He worked on this "comfort zone" of being in the same organization for years together; being at the same place, never wanting to change. While here was Vishi who had an aggressive travel schedule, who knew what it takes to work in different parts of the world. Who knew how to be successful despite going through a rough weather? The problem was not with Vishi, the problem was with her mentor who never understood the art of a "diversified working environment." Who had tremendously failed in his understanding about her?

Today Vishi was happy after winning a good sales deal. She was happy today for herself; she was back in the game. Most of all she was no more a second tier senior sales manager. She was satisfied and stood strong as a rock as always. The most important aspect here is to believe in oneself. Because the miracle of success can happen and it can be you!! Sometimes you have to pull life by its horns! "Those undeserved joys which come uncalled and make us more pleased than grateful are (the ones) that sing." Henry D Thoreau

Chapter 8

OVERCOMING THE OFFICE SPACE

Today when she was nominated as the Vice-President—Human Resources, everyone applauded her with warmth and grace. There was a unanimous happiness shared by everyone, readily acknowledging her effort, her proactive views and a mind with a deep vision. Her daring approach to change and the willingness to change surprised many, her sincerity to perform, to rise after she began to fall, was amazing. It was her innocence and simplicity that won everyone but deep inside even her best critiques envied her.

Why is Vidhushi simply special? Most of all, why is she always able to create an impact-question those who always smirked at her suggestions until yesterday. Everyone likes to talk about her and everyone narrates her example but how many lay the rules and act on these rules for themselves, as Vidhushi did. May be few or may be none. Few of us like to advice, as that's the easiest. Few of us try to execute but leave it mid-way as it requires to be disciplined but only a handful make things happen. Vidhushi was amongst that handful.

Vidhushi knows that nothing at all has been simple in this office space. She learnt the rules of the game, by being a participant herself. She had her share of hardships. There were times when the management meetings ruled out all her suggestions, termed her being defocused in her approach, found her an utter misfit to represent human resources as a profession and most of all—her critiques ensured she never makes the mark.

However, that was undermining her spirit and her daring temperament. She stood against all odds and learnt step by step. After all more than a decade of experience in leading companies cannot amount to a waste! With face to face with failure, Vidhushi accepted everything but stood firm to change for the better. She was young, enduring and above all remained cheerful all the time.

It was hard; initially it was against her grain to accept everything at the face value. She chalked out a plan for herself and termed it "overcoming the office space."

She began to think intensely where things were going wrong and why were they going wrong. Why was she missing every front and why were her suggestions never accepted. She knew this was affecting her appraisal, she also knew that she would not give up that easily.

She started with rule one that is to accept positive criticism gracefully but learn to defend oneself with facts and figures. There were times when enough was not conveyed but she was expected to perform. She knew that information was being held back. She knew there was communication barrier being created repeatedly.

However, here she learnt the second rule. To perform each task minutely and meticulously. To go in-depth of every problem and work towards macro management. As a result she was able to extract details after details and ensured that everything is read "in - between the lines." It was not just about basic learning; it was about being learned all the time and every time.

However, this was not enough there was still another rule she had to learn. To present her facts as they are and create a vision from her thought process. This was indeed difficult because this could pose challenge, this could encourage an inbuilt clash of ideas. She managed and she managed it well. Her methodology was simple—to stop working hard and to start working smart. So much so that her superiors were surprised to digest the information intake she provided them. The well-informed, grey haired wisdom stood challenged slowly and steadily.

The management meetings she attended were more than just the "figure gimmicks" it was becoming a self—learning ground. An arena where she had promised herself to make her mark. She knew the battle was tough, she knew she was alone but she also knew that she enjoys challenge.

She took upon herself the fourth rule-which was a sincere attempt towards self-improvement and trying to adapt oneself to the environment-as it is, not as she chooses it to be. This was most difficult. She now had to learn the techniques of the office—space.

She had to learn to know what to speak-when, where and how. She had to weigh her words, be precise in her though process, and ensure she concludes with an idea worth an "age-old wisdom." Most of all, she learnt the importance of acceptability and flexibility in these meetings. It was a hard - hitting word for her, but she had to learn to be shrewd.

No more would she just walk out of these meetings, or skip them because she disliked the constant criticism. No more, she would like to escape the burden of the challenge of "being—wrong all the time." However, come what may, she had decided not to quit. Though she knew she was youngest in these meeting but she also knew she would outsmart everyone one day.

Somehow the office space was becoming a challenging ground for her, each moment on every Monday at 830a.m. These meetings would last for hours and hours and she learnt that she had an important part to play. She had to carry her people with her. In addition, that brought her to the fifth rule.

There is nothing greater than teamwork. Vidhushi learnt to represent her team as a single entity undistorted by any argument. She learnt to represent their views, their thoughts as a Wholesome thought process. Slowly it was realized that her presentations were amazing. She brought forth such ideas which none in the meeting could envisage. She represented the employee and the business viewpoint in a complete balanced atmosphere that it took, hours to actually amount to a single criticism. In addition, there was no going back now.

Vidhushi improved, she tremendously changed. The time had come when employee forum would request her for presentation on macro human resources issues. She was rising above the ground of an annual appraisal or the annual compensation discussion. She was here to talk about issues, which deeply interested a large forum.

Her discussion involved the employee enthusiasm; the employees began to identify themselves with her views. So much so that the Monday 8.30a.m trauma, learnt to acknowledge her effort in a positive perspective. Her presentations were discussed with deep interest from all corners be it technical or marketing. The senior management began to identify the brilliant balance she brought between her thoughts and the company business plan. Afcourse this all demanded a lot of her personal time, in-depth case studies were read, plenty books were analyzed, surveys were performed.

However, amongst the many important things office space taught her to be strong and solid as the rock. To be unshaken by moments when one would lose her patience, she learnt the art of being "face to face with challenge" She learnt that it was initially difficult for her to sustain herself in the environment that's like a roller-coaster.

However, most of all she learnt that the final rule of self-sustenance is self-confidence. One cannot afford to be shaken away easily so much so that one has to accept, change, confront, and conclude. In addition, therein she learnt the fifth rule "being positive helps." As also there is no such thing as good or bad luck. Everything has a cause that produces appropriate effects. It might not be easy but surely it's not impossible to carve a pathway for oneself midst chaotic disorder. It might take time but after crawling or falling one does begin with the first step to walk ahead. If there is an urge to make the difference one can definitely bring a change with consistent effort. Having set the golden standard of self discipline, Vidhushi learnt to create and to build.

"Be not afraid of life. Believe that life is worth living, and your belief will help create the fact." William James

Chapter 9

IT'S ALL IN THE MIND

She enjoys and feels the success, which others observe and envy. From today she is the - International Marketing Head -of a leading software firm. A position well envied by her peers till yesterday, is a position she enjoys today. She is the sole recipient of the successful award, which the best in the company would yearn and struggle to earn. She had the rough weather as well. She is most happy to see herself succeed because this success was not easy at all. She is young and dynamic who believes in herself!

Nothing has been simple down this memory lane. Nothing has spared her either - bad politics within the organization, conscious effort to ensure she does not succeed by few, maneuverings of facts to let her down, constant criticism during the management meetings, simply to butcher her morale at times-but she has been fighting strong. She is like a pillar, totally unshaken by any storm. Today as she is in the position, she is unchallenged and unquestioned. She has proved her mettle as "nothing succeeds like success."

What everyone questions is why she is the best, though they are convinced about her potential? She is neither from the best Business School nor from a leading technology school. She has neither studied the management jargons taught and grilled in your sweat and blood, nor did she spend any time learning those algorithms or management theories. So what brings success akin to her? Luck afcourse but is it all about "being lucky" or is there a secret to this success?

Meet Maithli, an unassuming personality. Simple and soft, caring and a thoughtful planner today. She admits that nothing has been easy for her. Her job involves ample travel. She also has personal commitments to meet. Success is the leading edge in her life-but the key to success is a secret she discloses with pride. She has made many mistakes as like all of us but she learnt from them as alike, some of us. She made a deliberate attempt to change herself for the better, which we all as always work towards but leave it midway sometimes.

She's got her hands dirty doing that real basic stuff, which is considered monotony and lack of value addition to ones life. But it's important never to forget the basics, the grass roots, she feels. She laughs today, when her colleagues rate work as good and as bad. For her, work is work that requires a completion.

Quick results are best arrived at with clear planning. Being proactive is essential, she feels. Analyzing the data is her passion and as a result, she has facts and figures on her tips. She knows the pulse of the market as close to the beat of her heart. An aggressive reader, she extracts time from her everyday schedule to make things happen for her.

People, who have worked for her, rate her best. Management she feels is never taught, it comes with experience. To be the best in the field, besides self grooming, a self - discipline is essential. She has as others, learnt from past. She has learnt while she practiced. Opportunities didn't fall on her lap all of a sudden. She had to go through the acid test by the superiors, clear them and then was delegated responsibility. She is passionate about her people as also is business oriented. She is driven by this passion by one word-positive attitude and willingness to change for the better.

She might have lost the battle yesterday, but she is here to win the war. Success takes time, everything takes time to ripe, and she feels today. Therefore, what's essential is patience, which she has gathered over a period of time.

Maithli was most impatient in the early years of her career, she wanted to change things over night, but nothing happened. Infact during her first year of work experience, she received the worst rating in her appraisal. She was condemned for being impatient and running to conclusion without adequate analysis. Slowly she began to realize that, change is accepted and welcomed with interim phases. This experience slowly brings maturity in life. She learnt from her first rating, she ought to be patient and more analytical, if she wants a decent career to continue. Else, she is asking for trouble. Yes, she was learning the harder way.

Adaptability is what she felt was most important. In what ever environment was given to her, her first reaction was resistance. Resistance brought her constant criticism and built more critiques in the organization. Today she accepts how incorrect she was in showing resistance to almost every idea, every thought process-unless it involved rapid overnight change.

She admits being level headed and humble always pays in life. In her early years in the organization, she was known for her arrogance and over confidence. This might have helped her at times but definitely damaged her a lot. Until she was warned by her own boss—"to mend her behavior or quit."

This was a turning point for Maithli. From that day, she gave in her best to alter herself, her attitude to life, to people, to her environment.

Thereafter there was no looking back. She observed meticulous details about herself; she began to bring personality changes in herself. Initially it was difficult for her. She went wrong with same mistakes so many a times. Until she promised herself, never to repeat them. She admits it was incorrect on her part to learn the harder way; she should have been pro active and sensible.

When change began to occur, it all happened for the best. Her changed behavior surprised a many, but she was determined to succeed in bringing these personality changes which were harming her road to success. Maithli didn't learn this in any management school; she learnt it instead, from her environment, from her peers, from her superiors. She made a deliberate attempt to ensure things happen the right way, in a positive perspective. She did not quit instead, she changed herself, she did not give up instead took up this as a real challenge for herself.

Maithli changed, she completely changed herself. Her appraisal rating moved from average to good and then to excellent. She became an example to reckon with in the organization. She was quoted by her critiques as a determined person all set to bring a change one wonders about. She practiced over a period of time and learnt constantly to mould herself into a personality people adore today. She is ordinary but special, she is different and complete - from today she is the employee of the month in the organization. She has a reason to be what she is today, as it is all in the mind

- where half the battle is won or lost.

Chapter 10

HOW MUCH IS TOO MUCH

Ishwaran has been in a real dilemma since yesterday. She definitely understands that the opportunity in Uganda is excellent. It will contribute in her career growth, it will give her an excellent cultural perspective about working globally, and it would help her be the person she wants to be desires to be and would live up to be. However there are apprehensions. Plenty of them in terms of the cultural bias.

She has faced the problem of cultural diversity right here in USA; in countries in Europe. She has been on a learning curve with respect to low context and high context societies. But that's what the global corporate world is all about. Boston forced her to develop interest in Baseball against cricket whereas Germany compelled her to learn German as against her own mother tongue Bengali, Strange isn't it. Sometimes situations teach us how to prioritize our own interests, despite our unwillingness to do so. But that's life, I guess.

Iswaranan knows that her immediate boss is a tough nut to crack. His business focus compels him to drive the show more with a client focus than employee focus. As also she understands that not much can be done when the economy is not favorable. She knows getting the projects is an uphill task and not everyone's piece of cake. However what she doesn't understand is that she has bid the project for the company ADB Uganda, she is the project manager, she has been assigned a responsible team and most of all she heads the show.

It would be an excellent opportunity for her in terms of career growth, in terms of studying a different culture and understanding the horizons of diversity. Yes, she has her own apprehensions. However is there anything she can do to overcome these apprehensions though she knows that she is people and business focused? She is an excellent relationship manager. Most of all bidding for this project was such a great challenge for her. Her own boss had doubts if Iswaran would be capable to handle the deal but when she succeeded it amazed everyone. She was not only capable; she knew how to turn-around things.

Does Iswaran have an option, may be not. So today she packs her bag and head towards Uganda.

Her first day at the client had been a pleasant one as against what she thought. As time passed, Iswaran started getting fully engaged in her project. She had an excellent team coming from diverse cultures. Yes it tends to be challenging working with different type of personalities successfully.

Surely there were initial problems with the team to start with. It was not the language barrier it was the different personality types within the team that were becoming challenging to manage. To make matters worse, her client also started interfering in her thought process. Things were getting out of hand it seemed. But there was one thing happening smoothly that is the project was being implemented as per schedule.

Initially Iswaran faced criticism with respect to her communication, her inability to understand a diverse culture, her inability to adapt and handle her team together. However the client and her team knew that her knowledge power was amazing and she could not be challenged. Iswaran spend hours wondering during the course of the project implementation, what was practically going wrong. She knew there was a problem but could not identify, she knew she was struggling with herself most of the time. But why was all this happening? She is an experienced, hands on, intelligent person who has experienced different working environments. She knows the difference between comfort and discomfort but don't know the cause of it.

Why was she not able to adjust to this new environment? Was it the client, the team, the environment, the project or was it about herself this time. May be it was about herself. Iswaran stepped back and thought about the past events. She recalled the effort she had put in to sell this project to ADB Uganda. Despite major competitors none could compete with her statistics, her clarity and her vision to lead project. Her managing the project was a challenge for her, something that belonged to her and should end with her successful effort only. Iswaran had to make it happen somehow. But the question was how? Initially there were no answers to any of her queries, as though her thought process was getting blocked by her own perceptions and inhibitions.

As time passed things began to change. Iswaran began to realize that she had to make the "big change" before pointing a finger. She changed her strategy with respect to her client and her team. She slowly began to change from a "hard core task oriented manager to a participative manager."

She realized that her knowledge might help a successful implementation; however she also needed to establish a "lasting relation" with the client. Which meant her soft skills had to improve in the direction of understanding the cultural diversity? Being experienced she knew every individual is different, every place has its unique features and adapting to change is not easy either. What's easy is talking, giving sermons and most of all advising others on "how should they" as against "how they are."

Afcourse this process of change was not an overnight process; it took weeks for Iswaran to make this deliberate attempt to change herself, her working style, her managing style and most of all her thought process. She definitely made mistakes in the beginning but the effort she was making to bring the change was visible and as clear as crystal water. Characteristic of any project deliverable may be plenty of grape vine, how can these be ruled out attimes. One has to live with this spice in life also.

So did Iswaran begin to appreciate the so called world of "constructive criticism?" She knew she was neglected at times, her opinions were not welcomed warmly, and she felt ignored at times as well. Afcourse it was frustrating initially, she felt like tearing apart the whole project, packing her bags to leave. Or may be quit once and for all. But that was not wisdom at any cost, that was not her real self. The real world is not always welcoming and tender it has its bitter edges!

Having faced all these basic irritants the only option was "to change." May be it was the only alternative, the difficult alternative because what change welcomes with it is resistance also. Especially fighting for change within oneself is an exciting struggle. Not everyone can do it, face it and challenge oneself. It is not about submitting passively instead it is about making a deliberate attempt to improve oneself.

However she knew she could make the difference, she had the capacity. She also knew she would not give up. And when change was experienced and became visible it was like a feather in the hat. The client appreciated her, though hesitantly in the beginning but in course of time her smart working style was welcomed. Yes, recognition came to Iswaran not as a cake walk, it was difficult. She had to burn the midnight oil to ensure nothing goes wrong. At times she wondered was it worth it. However she also knew, to quit was not her temperament.

In course of time events began to speak for her smart working style. One could easily pierce through her potential and conclude on her exceptional intellect. Surely things changed for the better, positive thinking enabled Iswaran to see where the sun rises. She maintained a focus that helped the client and her team to achieve the ultimate objective i.e. a successfully satisfied deliverable. The entire project deliverable was handled well. The project was implemented as per the strict deadline. There was no delay at all. Yes, Iswaran and her team made it happen.

During the last day of their stay the client gave the entire team a warm farewell. A gathering one would seldom experience. There was rejoice, there was delight and most of all there was plenty of mutual appreciation. Above everything else, there was acknowledgement of effort, there was a deliberate attempt by the client business partner to ensure Iswaran and her team has a memorable farewell.

Somehow it was not all about a project alone, it was also about the people who wanted to make a special day for this entire team that had worked hard to make things happen. Until the business partner who was heading the client project addressed the gathering. He complemented the team for its successful delivery, for its patience and the ability to make things happen. However it didn't end here. He had lots to mention about Ishwaran that surprised her delightfully. It brought her greater happiness because she never expected this warmth. It never happened in the past and here she was being welcomed and recognized as never before. She wondered to herself if this actually happens in the corporate world, but the reality was it was happening, all in front of her. Yes, it was real as clear as the daylight.

The client was pleased with the contribution of the team and so was Ishwarans manager. Everyone was happy with this success but the only person in real turmoil was Iswaran. She realized that her initial apprehensions were nothing but her preconceived notions, her false perceptions which clouded her thinking completely. The project in ADB Uganda was learning for life that she should not get bias with her environment even before she experiences it. Getting bias effects the thought process and overrules setting the right direction for one maybe. Afcourse there is bias everywhere but having this feeling overrule ones focus and reason can be unhealthy. Experiencing success after this personal struggle internally Iswaran realized "understanding is indeed the beginning of approving." Andre Gide.

Chapter 11

THE UNCOOKED FEAST

Pranay was the project leader for the client Time Is Money. He had a history of successful implementations, with an excellent client feedback. He had deep knowledge with a strong technical acumen. A strong personality with a focused thought process. Pranay was an ideal combination of an in-depth personality who was task and people driven. In the past his peers, his team, his mentor had praised him for his work and accomplishments. It was not easy to compete with Pranay not because he would crush his competitor but because his humility would overpower an arrogant mind easily. But today is not the same.

Today Pranay reports as a project leader into his mentor, things are also not the same. His mentor comes from a different cultural background. Though not as deep in knowledge as Pranay, he definitely gets an edge because he is identified well with the client. He speaks the same language and has the same cultural heritage. But could this effect work, definitelty not, thought Pranay. It was too narrow overview if he believed in this thought process. For a moment Pranay overlooked this matter completely. He had a different outlook to understand people. Barriers as ethnicity, language, heritage could surely not effect work, he was confident.

Well that was what Pranay thought. In course of time, he started seeing a visible difference between the client's attitude to his mentor and himself. His mentor took a lead be it in meetings, or social gatherings or making presentations or even explaining the basics to the client. Pranay was a background artist to manage the project and his team. He was not encouraged to participate with the client nor was he required to get any visibility. Why were things going out of hand, Pranay wondered to himself? He had excellent work credentials, client feedback from varied countries, but that was his past.

The present is totally different; it's almost a visible black patch of stagnation where there seems no lateral thinking leave aside career progression. What does pranay do, it's hard for him to pick up Japanese language or even develop a taste for Japanese food for that matter. Or has he lost, he wont be successful in this project because of an ethnic barrier. Will he have to work like a paid laborer whose task is to simply do the basic tasks without value adding to the project? However Pranay had to find a way out.

In the beginning he let the way things would go. He let his mentor take the lead and enjoy the optimum visibility like the sun during summer time. Definitely it was frustrating for Pranay, more so when his best presentations were conducted by his mentor. Upset and anguished Pranay decided to take one week leave from work.

He wanted to rethink on his career, implore if it was worth pursuing with the organization under the current conditions. He cannot believe his past independent of present, surely he has been successful in the past, everyone has been appreciative of his work and he always thought that would be a guiding force for the present moment. But things were totally different. There was nothing as worse as being ignored.

All looked so much worse each time he thought of the project, his mentor or even the client. However Pranay could not conclude on anything, with the current economic scenario he had little courage to take unnecessary chances with his career unless the opportunity was brilliant. It was no point to quit a job. There were no projects where he could take a shift. Practically he was stuck and either he could make it happen or let things be the way they are. His appraisal would smile with one more implementation to his credit. That was not a satisfying thought at all.

Well Pranay joined back work from leave. He continued to work at his best thinking one day his smart work would payback.

Things were not the same when he came back from leave. The project was at an utter chaotic stage, there was lack of quality work going on, the client seemed dissatisfied by his mentor and everything was totally disoriented. So much of a change in a week's time surprised him. He never imagined things could be so different i.e. so much worse in his absence?

However at this stage Pranay changed his work strategy. He discussed in detail about his role with the mentor and clearly told him he would like to handle this chaotic stage of project all by himself. He would like to take the lead. Well his mentor had no option but to agree. He knew if the project continued as this for another week the entire team might get rolled out.

Pranay knew it was challenging to manage the project at this stage, he also knew if he was able to handle now, he would handle it for the rest of its duration. He spends hours working towards each module and practically did a quality testing at every stage. He never realized his absence could make so much of a difference.

When Pranay encountered the client, things started to improve and to change. His proposals had content which could not be disputed and his confidence gave client the reminder that he was a critical member of the team who could no longer be ignored. His knowledge was his power, slowly the client also realized that Pranay might be from a different ethnic background; still at heart he was a warm, loving person, who was polite and humble. Who had strong business acumen and the maturity to handle crisis. He was not here on a giving up mode, instead he was here to improve things.

His absence could make such a massive difference was amazing to the client as also to his mentor. His mentor might never have acknowledged his contribution but he knew that without Pranay the project was in a real crisis mode. He also knew that he lacked the intellect and creativity of Pranay, he would admit only to one person that is "himself."

Pranay also decided that he would no longer sit at the background and get frustrated any more. He made a deliberate attempt to ensure he gets the visibility, his knowledge is well acknowledged, his presence is well appreciated and most of all he is heard. He is not considered a silent spectator to a meeting or a gathering. Pranay slowly became an extreme extrovert, he began to pierce his way, he learnt to make things happen for himself this time. And there was no giving up now. He would not sit back in isolation or call his peers to share his experience. Instead he would give direction to events the way he wanted and move in the desired role. More so when there was an opportunity to do so.

In course of time he ensured that the Project met its deadline and was implemented successfully. Yes it was almost done single handedly. His ideas were amazing and his scientific approach to measure the pros and cons to a situation was worth learning. His contribution was so unique to the project that the client partner wanted him to manage and not lead another project. He was in few days time impressed by Pranay, he realized the immense mistake he made by not interacting with Pranay in the past.

Yes this project changed Pranay as a person. It didn't make him arrogant or stubborn instead it made him realize that at times one needs to pierce through the crowd with ones effort and smart thinking. Most of all it always helps to be patient and positive no matter how slippery is the pathway. He might not have still learnt Japanese or even developed an interest in Japanese cuisine but did it really matter?

He learnt to be what he was lacking all this while, that is to be shrewd not always but sometimes when the situation demands. There are times when one has to say "no" rather than saying "yes" all the time. There are times when one has to say "enough is enough." May be because "you never know what is enough unless you know what is more than enough." William Blake.

Chapter 12

FROM SCHEDULES TO DINING

Ayesha understands the importance of success. Success brings her confidence and happiness, her adrenal keeps her competitive appetite nourished and blooming.

She begins her day early morning and ends it late. The weekend ends in planning or strategizing business plan for the finance division of her company. She has designed her routine to her convenience and her desire which alienates herself from her friends or her own family sometimes. She has everything but time for herself today.

She has completed series of successful projects in the past, has risen her profit centre to a remarkable level, surely none can compete her potential or talent. Her creativity and exposure to a working environment is diverse and she appreciates and understands the challenges involved in heading a profit centre, in creating and building successfully.

Surely Ayesha has a sound knowledge of work and partially her own life in general. She is happy at work but lately she is not been satisfied with herself.

It's difficult for her to identify the problem, though she has the art of striking the target and resolving the issue on the work front. The moment she knows the pulse of the problem diagnosis is easy and quick. She doesn't understand what's making her dissatisfied, as though she is yearning for a change that she is unable to identify or conclude upon. She seems to be standing on the crossroads of her life today, where she has an over nourished bank balance to offer her a comfortable living but not a satisfying living.—Till yesterday she understood both these terms as a single entity but today there is a cloud of difference. So what is the disturbing point today?

What is creating the uneasiness in her lately, she has never been as this in the past. She has always identified herself as a person who is mature and can handle large issues, who can create a complex matrix to resolve an issue and council professionals.

Is she again mixing her approach at handling activities in office with the home front? Her successful repetitive thought processes at the office is just not churning any success in her personal life. Her personal life needs to differ from her professional life. It's not about the complex financial matrix nor it's about articulating a methodology that works well in a working environment. So what is the problem?

What can quench her thirst to both a happy and a satisfying living? Surely she has to make the final attempt to identify the cause. The disturbing point that's leading her to a serious thinking about herself, her schedules and most of all her life in general. There are times when one is unable to identify the problem accurately. There are another times when the problem is identifiable but we overlook the impact it is creating unless we are the affected.

After ample imploring she felt that the disturbing point has been her constant observation about Rahim, her son. Yes Rahim has stopped complaining. Rahim has not asked her for long to take a break from work for a vacation. Neither has he expressed a desire for skiing this season. A sport he can't imagine missing during the season. He understands that he has a schedule to follow and has his peers to keep him occupied with games. So was this developing distance from Rahim a disturbing point for Ayesha. May be yes. This was impacting her as a person. A sense of guilt each time she would come home late from a meeting or schedule or even attending a conference call during the weekends. Her life was coming to a point where she needed to hault for a while and rethink the strong momentum with which she wanted to lead a life. She was definitely not satisfied but lately she began to be unhappy as well. So what does Ayesha do?

The next afternoon Ayesha was back from work and she engaged herself in the daily chores of home. Yes the house where she was living till yesterday seemed a home in just a matter of few hours. Until Rahim was back from school and was surprised to see his mother home during the day light. It was delightful for him. Ayesha and Rahim sat together over lunch, they spend the evening together and had great fun during dinner. These few hours were fulfilling for both. Though it was simple, but the best dinner relished together. Next day onwards Ayesha repeated the same routine. She realized that she would spend weekends with Rahim and that was what she termed her "family time."

She also decided to take a fortnight leave from work and explore Vermont for Skiing. The time she was spending with Rahim seemed the best time ever. Rahim seemed joyous, satisfied and full of life. Little did Ayesha realize she had so much to discover about her son. His tales and experiences during the skiing surprised her; it was as though he had to complete sharing innumerable experiences within a moment.

Slowly she began to discover that there was more to life than those meeting schedules or receiving the best employee awards. Those were essential nodoubt but not as important as this moment she was spending with her son. Coming back from vacation Ayesha decided to change her outlook to life. She decided to balance her time between work and bedtime stories, between conference calls and interesting cuisines and most of all understanding that she needed to be both happy and satisfied, being happy alone was not enough nor was being satisfied alone a complete process by itself.

Things changed for the better. Surely she realized the close bond developing between herself and Rahim. She could have probably missed those critical moments to observe him grow as a person had she been drowned in the pile of files or meetings or constant business travel.

Afcourse bringing this balance was difficult and challenging initially. Sometimes she felt she was neglecting work at times she felt she was ignoring Rahim. But each time she was convinced that bringing the balance was not easy either. However it was better than before. Lives seemed meaningful and complete both back at home and at work. Ayesha might not have been able to strike a complete balancing act but definitely she made the difference with changing her perspective to her home and work life. Its only when she stopped living her office in her house, did she begin to get the feeling of being at home.

Incourse of time she ensured she is able to spend ample time with Rahim. She is able to make the most of the weekends, is able to mould her routine with flexibility where there is time to relax and sometimes if not always take life slightly easily. Ayesha did not make any dramatic change, her key change was the initiative to manage her time well between work and home.

Well she seemed a much satisfied and a happy person. Rahim was most happy to see his mother come home on time after work, in being with him and in belonging to him not just as a person who is available to guide and to help but as a warm bond that is to be nurtured forever. It was not about creating a miracle instead it was about little moments which sometimes we begin to neglect ourselves not realizing that there is more to life than scheduled meetings." Inside myself is a place where you live all alone, and that's where you renew your springs that never dry up."

Pearl S Buck

ABOUT THE AUTHOR

Sanjna S Katyal has been in the human resources field for a decade. Formerly she worked in Asea Brown Boveri, IBM, Adobe Systems, Smithkline Beecham and the Tata group of companies. Her extensive knowledge in human resources inspired her to establish InSearch, which she heads today. InSearch is a solution provider in human resources for the corporate world. InSearch can be visited at www.insearchglobal.com.

A post graduate in Human Resources from Delhi University, India Ms Katyal enjoys composing poetry. She is the recipient of the human resources award from National Institute of Personnel Management, India.

She lives with her spouse Arjun in New Jersey, USA. She considers Arjun as a key to her inspirational strength always inculcating in her the force to rejuvenate her creative talent and forceful thinking.

Her family is based in India. She is grateful to her family for being a powerful guiding force to her in motivating her intellect and talent. In developing a perspective that nourishes a personality.

www.ingramcontent.com/pod-product-compliance
Lightning Source LLC
Chambersburg PA
CBHW020336290526
45785CB00005B/2043